the munchies eatbook

or how to satisfy the hungries
without eating everything
in sight

the munchies eatbook

or how to satisfy the hungries without eating everything in sight.

written, illustrated and designed by

alice & eliot hess

VINTAGE BOOKS
A Division of Random House
New York

VINTAGE BOOKS EDITION 1973

Copyright © 1973 by Alice and Eliot Hess

Library of Congress Cataloging in Publication Data

Hess, Alice, 1949–
The munchies eatbook.

1. Cookery. I. Hess, Eliot, 1946–   joint
author. II. Title.
TX715.H5723   641.5'3   73-8759
ISBN 0-394-71924-7

Manufactured in the United States of America

Conceived by us while caught in the inescapable jaws of the Munchies.

Dedicated to those who have been there, who are there now, or who may be there soon.

contents

contents

the
munchies eatbook

or how to satisfy the hungries
without eating everything
in sight

introduction

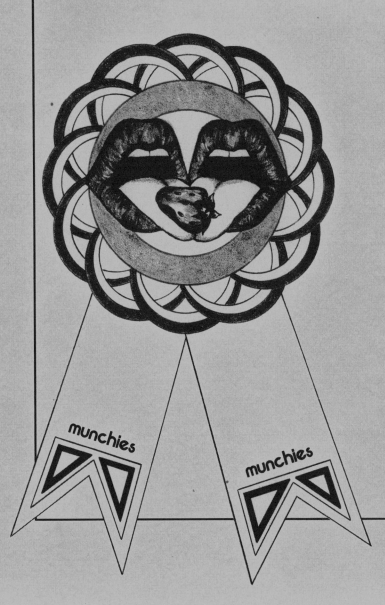

the official
munchies
seal of
approval

All recipes in this Eatbook are **OFFICIAL MUNCHIE TESTED RECIPES** and have been found to be 1st Quality Munchie Satisfiers by our select board of expert judges and contributors, including:

LORIE
PHYLLIS and LEWIS
DONNA
PETER and SUSAN
ROBERT
PENNY and EDDIE
LENNY
DAVID and CARLA
BUBIE
KENNY and DOROTHY
TIPPIE
JERRY and MARGIE
SALLY
PAUL and LINDA
RUSSELL J.
DAVE and HONEY
ROBBIE
KAREN and DAVID
STEVEN
MOM and DAD
LIL
MOM and DAD
     and MARTY our chief tester and
     spiritual advisor

WHAT ARE THE MUNCHIES?

The Munchies are a phenomenon that can be linked to many causes but that always manifest themselves in an uncontrollable desire to fill one's face with edible objects of abundant number and wild variety.

The intent of this book is to provide a directory for those who have been struck by the Munchies and are in a momentary state of panic, not knowing how to satisfy them.

Read this book carefully and pluck from it the recipes that tantalize your eye and titillate your tongue at a given moment. Don't be afraid to try any recipe. Some may sound strange, and some may look strange when prepared, but all aim to bring you to that state of being commonly called oral satisfaction, or the state of the **PEACEFUL PALATE**.

the peaceful palate

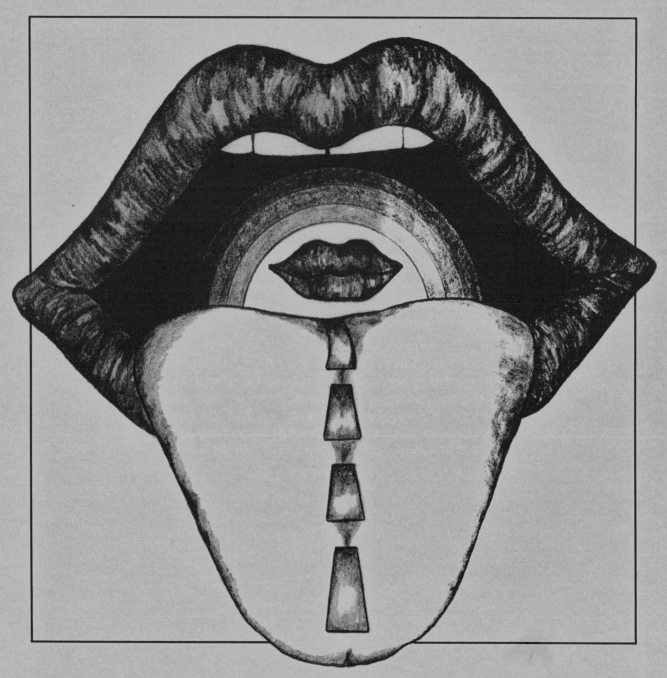

IN THE PURSUIT OF PACIFYING YOUR PALATE

1. **Eating in Circles.** Munchies come in varying degrees of attack: Common, Super, Colossal and Supreme. It has been our experience that a Colossal or Supreme attack often produces a secondary phenomenon, which we call **EATING IN CIRCLES.**

Example: You're pleasantly pursuing a particular Munchie craving, when suddenly your desires shift to something more appealing, then maybe a third, fourth, or fifth craving follows. Eventually, you're back to your original craving and quickly proceeding to repeat all the others, one by one, in the same exact order. How long you continue this cycle depends completely upon your capacity, which becomes enormously enlarged, or by your ability to close your mouth, shut your eyes, and repeat over and over, "Enough, enough, enough."

2. **Use all your senses.** Eagerly examine the infinite intricacies of a lettuce leaf. Leisurely listen to the classic crunch of a carrot. Subtly savor the scent of cinnamon. Frequently fondle your favorite fruit.

3. **Be prepared.** Since the Munchies can attack at any time, we suggest you always have the necessary ingredients to prepare your favorite Munchie dishes. This will facilitate their immediate preparation and subsequent consumption, and also prevent the necessity of going to the supermarket.
Warning: With great experience in such matters, we feel that the supermarket and the Munchies are definitely an unadvisable combination. Wheeling a shopping cart down endless aisles of lusciously stacked food enhances your Munchies unbelievably, promoting the purchase of a profusion of products you'll later wonder why you ever bought.

and now the munchies...

cravings
cravings
cravings
cravings
cravings
cravings
cravings
cravings
cravings
cravings
ravings
vings
ings
ngs
ns

sweet cravings

Munchies come in several flavors. The most common is Sweet. It is also the happiest and most pleasing to the everyday Muncher. Therefore, as a convenience to the majority of Munchers, we have started this book with that flavor.

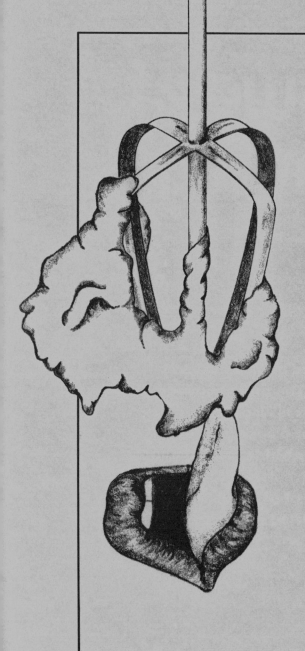

PLAIN OLD DELICIOUS HOMEMADE WHIPPED CREAM

Whip up a ½ pint of **heavy cream** and gradually beat in 4 tablespoons **sugar** and 1 teaspoon **vanilla.** Beat until fluffy, being careful not to overdo it or the resulting mixture will be a flavored butter. Any flavored extract can be substituted for the vanilla.

CHOCOLATE WHIPPED CREAM

Add 2 tablespoons **cocoa** while beating.

CINNAMON WHIPPED CREAM

Add ¼ teaspoon **cinnamon** while beating.

ORANGE WHIPPED CREAM

Substitute 2 tablespoons **orange juice concentrate** for vanilla.

SPIKED WHIPPED CREAM

Substitute 2 tablespoons **rum, brandy** or any **liqueur** for vanilla.

ice cream super sundaes

One of the most common Munchie Sweet Cravings is **ice cream.** Most Munchers have a favorite flavor. Many Munchers also like to mix their flavors, creating new and exciting variations, and add toppings: **chocolate sauce, butterscotch, walnuts, raisins, marshmallow, pretzels, preserves, fresh fruit, cookies, candies,** just about anything that tastes good and doesn't stifle the ice cream flavor. On top of the toppings the true Muncher will always leave room for **whipped cream** (see opposite page) which may be adorned with **chocolate sprinkles, multicolored sprinkles, shredded coconut, chocolate chips** or all of these. As the very last gesture, gently add a big, red, juicy **maraschino cherry.**

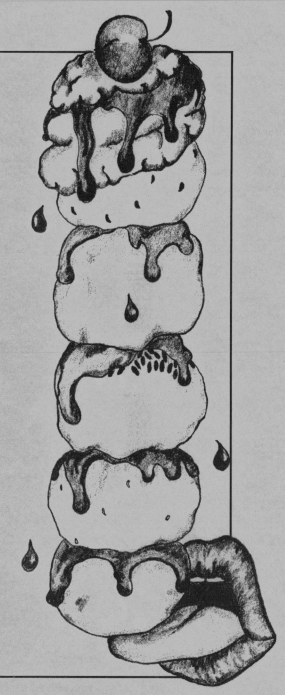

chocolate chips

CHOCOLATE CHIPS, PEANUT BUTTER AND MARSHMALLOW

Take a spoon and scoop out a reasonable portion of **peanut butter.** One by one, push **chocolate chips** into the peanut butter until there isn't room for any more. Now dip the spoon with the peanut butter and chocolate chips in a jar of **marshmallow sauce.** Take little nibbles or, if brave, swallow the whole spoonful at once.

chocolate chips

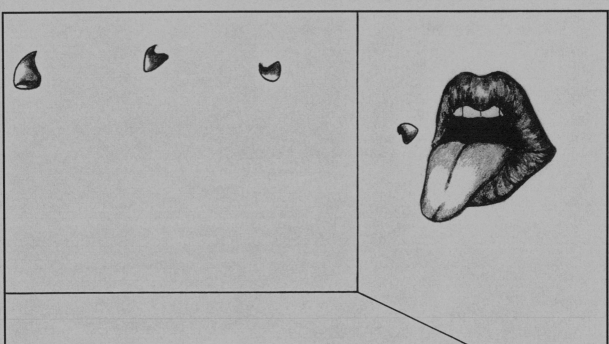

CHOCOLATE CHIPS AND COCONUT

This recipe is an exercise in perfectly coordinated eating rhythm.

Take a comfortable bite of **coconut** and chew, getting into a rhythmic up-and-down motion. When you're really into the taste of the coconut and it's evenly distributed throughout your mouth, take one **chocolate chip** and, at the precise moment your mouth is in an open position, pop it in and continue to chew. Repeat the process for extended satisfaction.

Fresh coconut is ideal if you want to bother to smash open a coconut. If not, shredded coconut is also quite good, although the taste is slightly different.

strawberries

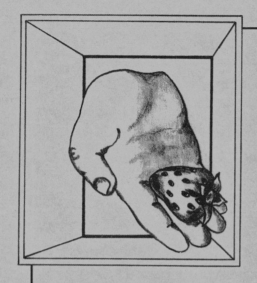

HONEY-COATED STRAW-BERRIES WITH WALNUTS

Remove the leaves and stems from as many **strawberries** as you feel like eating. Put them in a bowl, pour some **honey** on them and add **shelled walnuts.**

CHOCOLATE STRAWBERRIES

Try dipping fresh **strawberries** in melted chocolate from a **chocolate bar.**

strawberries

HOW TO EAT FRESH STRAWBERRIES—A NEAT TREAT

One cup of **strawberries**
One cup of **water**
One cup of **sugar**
A **paper napkin**

This recipe requires the use of only one hand. We leave it up to you to find a use for the other.

Pick up a **strawberry** by its stem and submerge it in the cup of **water.** Roll the wet berry in the **sugar** until it is thoroughly coated. Raise the strawberry to your mouth, bite and enjoy. Be careful not to consume the leaf and stem. They should be left intact and carefully placed on the waiting **paper napkin.** This process is repeated until all the berries are gone and all the leaves and stems are neatly left on the napkin. Fold the napkin and wipe your mouth with it.

PEACHES SPIKED WITH BRANDY

In a large bowl put 1 large can of drained **peach halves.** Pour in 2 tablespoons of **brandy** and mix. Combine 1 cup of **whipped cream** with ½ cup **sour cream,** 2 tablespoons **sugar** and 1 tablespoon **vanilla.** Pour into the bowl and sprinkle **chocolate chips** on the top. Serve with as many spoons as. people, or go off into a corner and eat the whole thing yourself.

peaches

PAULIE'S PERFECT PEACHES

Put a **peach half** in a dish. Place a ball of **vanilla ice cream** on top. Cover with thawed **frozen strawberries.** To make it perfect, top with **whipped cream.**

PEACHES AND CREAM—A WHOLESOME DISH

Take fresh **peaches** in season or drained canned peaches and slice thin. Spoon **whipped cream** on top and sprinkle with **shredded coconut** or a handful of **chocolate chips.**

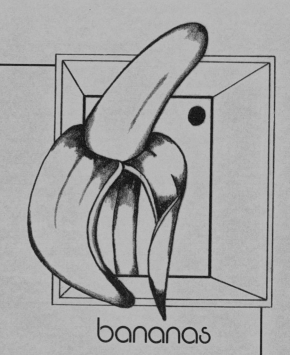

bananas

THE TOTAL BANANA EXPERIENCE

Melt **butter** in a frying pan. Cut **bananas** in half lengthwise. Sprinkle with **sugar** (brown or white) mixed with a little **cinnamon**. Add a squeeze of **lemon juice**. Fry until bananas are lightly browned. Turn and sprinkle again with cinnamon and sugar and brown. Serve with **ice cream** if desired.

BANANAS 'N CRUMBS

Cut 1 **banana** into approximately 1″ pieces. Dip pieces into a bowl that contains 1 beaten **egg.** Then roll in **cornflake crumbs.** Drop into deep fat and fry 2 minutes.

A BANANA SWEETIE

Slice a **banana** lengthwise about halfway through. Open and stick pieces of a **chocolate bar** along the cut. Place **miniature marshmallows** on top of the chocolate. Wrap the whole banana in aluminum foil and cook over a campfire or bake in an oven until the marshmallow melts.

bananas

BANANA, HONEY!

Cut **banana** in half lengthwise. Place flat side down in a greased baking pan. Spread with **honey** and add a good squeeze of **lime juice** and some **cinnamon.** Bake at 400° for 10–15 minutes. Baste with the juice drippings.

O.J. BANANA

Cut **banana** in half lengthwise. Dip in **orange juice** so that the banana is covered. Then roll in **shredded coconut** and place in a greased baking pan. Bake at 400° for 10–15 minutes. Baste with the juice drippings. Sprinkle with **cinnamon** or **nutmeg.**

TWO BANANAS ARE BETTER THAN ONE

BANANA ONE: Spread **peanut butter** on a **banana** and roll in **chopped walnuts.**

BANANA TWO: Slice **bananas** and top with **peanut butter** and 1 **chocolate chip.**

BANANA AND MARSHMALLOW

Slice **bananas** and put a **marshmallow** on top. Put in the oven until the marshmallow melts.

POWERFUL PRUNES

Stuff large **dried prunes** with **cream cheese** mixed with **walnuts**.

MESSAGE: After much deliberation and experimentation we have found it best to set a limit of ½ dozen of the above. Anyone who proceeds beyond that limit, does so at his or her own risk.

PRUNES SPREAD WITH CRUNCHY PEANUT BUTTER

This recipe speaks for itself.

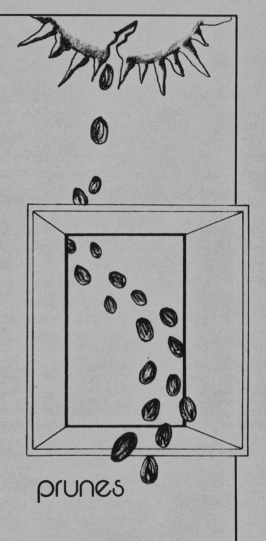

prunes

MY MOTHER'S SWEET APRICOTS

Blend 1 large chilled can of drained **apricots** until smooth. Cover completely with **whipped cream** and **strawberries** that have been rolled in **sugar** or dipped in **honey.**

APRICOTS AGAIN

Put **walnuts** on top of **whipped cream** that has been made with **rum** on the top of **apricot halves.**

APRICOT, MARSHMALLOW, APRICOT

Make a sandwich of **dried apricot halves** and **marshmallows.**

apricots

HOW TO EAT APPLES AND CHOCOLATE —A UNIFYING EXPERIENCE

Take one cold crisp **apple** in one hand, one neatly unwrapped **chocolate bar** fresh from the freezer in the other. Proceed by taking one bite of apple, then one of the chocolate bar, and chew together.

APPLE ADVENTURE

Pour the contents of a large can of **apple pie filling** into a bowl. Add a few tablespoons of **sugar** and sprinkle with **cinnamon** and **lemon juice** to taste. Top the filling with **whipped cream** and sprinkle with **nutmeg.**

apples

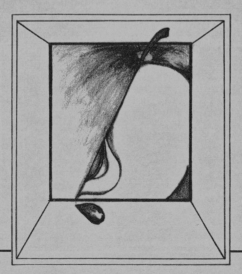

apples

RING AROUND YOUR APPLESAUCE

Pour the contents of 1 medium-size jar of **applesauce** into a saucepan. Add 1 **cinnamon stick,** sprinkle with **nutmeg** and heat over a small flame. Pour it into a bowl and place 1 red **spiced apple ring** in the center. Raise the bowl slowly to your lips, positioning them directly above the hole in the apple ring. Now start a vacuum action with your mouth and proceed to remove all the applesauce from the bowl by way of the hole. When all the applesauce has gone down, eat the apple ring.

PINEAPPLE APPLESAUCE WITH SPIRIT

Take 1 large jar of **applesauce** and add 1 small can of **crushed pineapple,** 4 tablespoons **sugar,** a small blob of **sour cream** and a small wine glass of **white wine.** Mix all the ingredients together and chill as long as it takes you to refill the wine glass and leisurely empty it.

pineapple

SO YOU WANT TO GO TO HAWAII

Put **pineapple slices** side by side in a shallow baking dish. Pour ½ the juice from the can over the slices. Fill each hole with **maraschino cherries,** sprinkle with **brown sugar** and put under the broiler for 5 minutes. Remove from baking dish and place in bowls. Sprinkle with **shredded coconut** and **chocolate chips.** Now sit back, think about palm trees, eat all the fruit, then drink all the juice, get out your ukulele and sing one chorus of **HONO-LULU BABY**.

orange and

grapefruit

WHAT TO DO WITH AN ORANGE

Peel an **orange** and cut the slices into small pieces. Mix with **orange** or **raspberry sherbet.** Add **maraschino cherries, shelled walnuts** and **whipped cream.**

GRILLED GRAPEFRUIT

Halve and section a **grapefruit** and leave in shell. Spread **honey** liberally on each half. Sprinkle with **sugar** and top with a **maraschino cherry.** Brown in broiler under a medium flame until lightly golden in color.

pears and grapes

PEARS SPIKED WITH RUM

Put a canned **pear half** in a shallow baking pan. Pour on **honey** and sprinkle with **lemon juice**. Take a bottle of **rum** and add a little. Detach yourself from the bottle and put the pan into a 350° oven for about 10 minutes. Before eating, turn the pear over and baste with the savory juices.

GRAPES DELICIOUS

Over a bunch of **seedless white grapes** pour some **white wine**. Throw on a blob of **sour cream, brown sugar** and **cinnamon**.

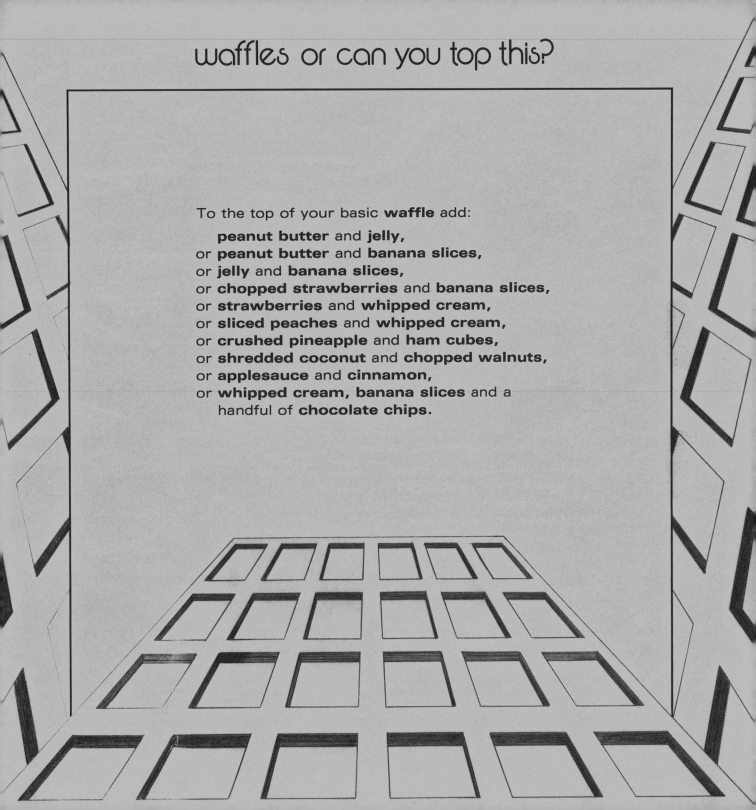

waffles or can you top this?

To the top of your basic **waffle** add:

peanut butter and **jelly,**
or **peanut butter** and **banana slices,**
or **jelly** and **banana slices,**
or **chopped strawberries** and **banana slices,**
or **strawberries** and **whipped cream,**
or **sliced peaches** and **whipped cream,**
or **crushed pineapple** and **ham cubes,**
or **shredded coconut** and **chopped walnuts,**
or **applesauce** and **cinnamon,**
or **whipped cream, banana slices** and a
handful of **chocolate chips.**

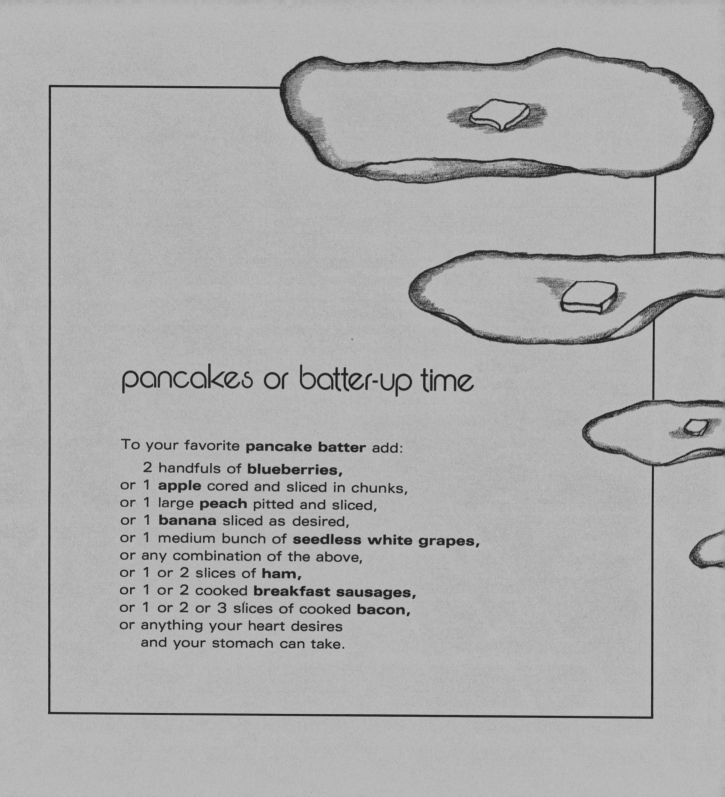

pancakes or batter-up time

To your favorite **pancake batter** add:

    2 handfuls of **blueberries,**
or 1 **apple** cored and sliced in chunks,
or 1 large **peach** pitted and sliced,
or 1 **banana** sliced as desired,
or 1 medium bunch of **seedless white grapes,**
or any combination of the above,
or 1 or 2 slices of **ham,**
or 1 or 2 cooked **breakfast sausages,**
or 1 or 2 or 3 slices of cooked **bacon,**
or anything your heart desires
    and your stomach can take.

NOODLE PANCAKE OR THE NEBULOUS NOODLE WHO IN HIS SEARCH FOR TRUE IDENTITY BECAME A PANCAKE

Take 2 cups of **cooked noodles, 2 eggs,** a handful of **softened raisins***and 1 teaspoon of **salt.** Mix together in a bowl until they are well acquainted with each other, then pour the whole crowd into a **buttered** frying pan and brown on both sides. Sprinkle with **sugar** and serve.

* A **softened raisin** is a raisin that has had its wrinkles removed by the simple operation of soaking in water, thereby causing its skin to be as soft as it used to be when it was a young grape.

FLIPPED-OUT APPLE FLAPJACKS

Peel 1 large **apple** and cut it into small cubes. Make a mixture of 3 **eggs** and ½ cup **sugar,** add 1 cup **milk,** ¾ cup **flour** and 1 teaspoon **baking powder.** Combine the apples and the mixture and spoon into a **buttered** frying pan, making small circles about the size of an Australian wombat's paw. (If a wombat is not handy, try to approximate 2".) Fry till brown, flip and brown again. Mix some **cinnamon** and **sugar** together and sprinkle on top.

toasts

CINNAMON TOAST

Melt 4 tablespoons **butter** in pan. Add 1 teaspoon **cinnamon** and 5 tablespoons **sugar**. Spread on toast, roll or muffin.

OPTIONAL: For a chocolate flavor, add ½ cup **cocoa** to the mix or sprinkle with **chocolate chips.**

COCOA TOAST

Melt 4 tablespoons **butter** in pan. Add 6 tablespoons **cocoa** and 5 tablespoons **sugar**. Spread on toast, roll or muffin.

OPTIONAL: For a little spice, sprinkle some **cinnamon** on top.

FRENCH CORN TOAST

To an 8-ounce can of **creamed corn** add 1 **egg** and a little **milk.** Soak a slice of **white** or **whole wheat bread** in the mixture. Fry in a pan with **butter,** browning both sides. Sprinkle with **salt** and **pepper,** cover with **maple syrup.**

FIXED-UP CORN MUFFINS

Cut a **corn muffin** in half, spread with **butter, honey, walnuts** and **sugar** and put under the broiler.

FRENCH TOAST NUMBER ONE

Beat 2 **eggs** with ½ cup **milk** and ½ teaspoon **vanilla.**
Soak **white** or **whole wheat bread** in the mixture. Fry
in **butter** and serve with **raisins, brown sugar, cinnamon** and **maple syrup.**

FRUITY FRENCH TOAST

Beat 2 **eggs** with ½ cup of any **fruit nectar** and 1 heaping tablespoon of **honey.** Soak **white** or **whole wheat
bread** in the mixture. Fry in **butter** and serve with **sugar**
or **maple syrup** or **honey.**

MAXWELL'S MILK TOAST

Soak pieces of **white** or **whole wheat bread** in **sweetened condensed milk** and sprinkle with **shredded
coconut** and **chocolate chips.** Bake on greased pan
or aluminum foil in 350° oven for 10–15 minutes.

BUBIE'S CHOCOLATE CAKE

This cake is 100% guaranteed to hook you from the first bite to the last. Many is the time we've sat down for a slice and completely demolished the whole cake. BEWARE!

Sift together   2¼ cups **flour,** ½ cup **cocoa,**
                   1½ teaspoons **baking soda** and
                   1½ teaspoons **baking powder.**
Beat together 5 **eggs,** ¾ cups **liquid shortening,**
                   2 teaspoons **vanilla** and gradually
                   add 2 cups **sugar.**
Mix dry and liquid ingredients together. Add 1½ cups **hot black coffee** and beat. Bake at 350° for 1 hour in a tube pan.

CHOCOLATE GLAZE FOR BUBIE'S CHOCOLATE CAKE

Mix together 1 cup **powdered sugar,** 3 tablespoons **cocoa,** 2 tablespoons **melted butter,** 2 teaspoons **vanilla** and 1–3 tablespoons **hot water** depending on desired consistency.

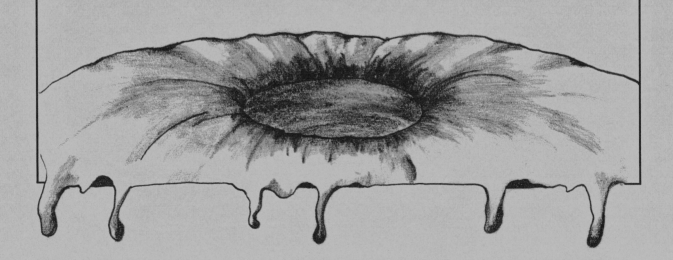

cookies

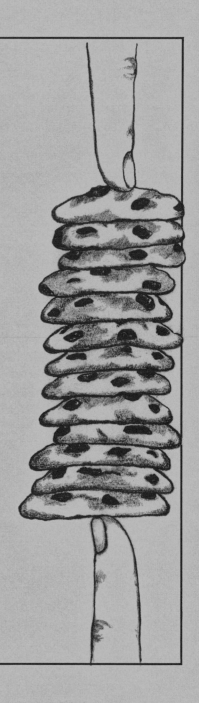

BUBIE'S CHOCOLATE CHIP COOKIES

This recipe makes lots of cookies. We like them. In fact, everybody likes them, especially with a tall glass of cold milk.

Sift together 2¼ cups **flour,** ½ teaspoon **salt,** ¼ teaspoon **baking powder** and ½ teaspoon **baking soda.**

Beat together 1 cup **shortening,** ½ cup **brown sugar,** ½ cup **sugar,** 1 teaspoon **vanilla,** 1 tablespoon **cold water** and 2 **eggs.**

Mix everything together. Stir in a large package of **chocolate chips.** Drop onto a **greased** cookie sheet by the teaspoonful and bake at 375° for 10–12 minutes.

CAMPFIRE COOKIE RECIPE

On a **graham cracker** put a piece of chocolate from a **chocolate bar.** Toast a **marshmallow** and put it on top of the chocolate. Finish it off with another **graham cracker.**

CHOCOLATE COOKIES WITH CREAM CHEESE

Spread **cream cheese** on top of **chocolate wafer cookies.**

PEANUT BUTTER CHOCOLATE CHIP

Spread **peanut butter** over your favorite **chocolate chip cookies.**

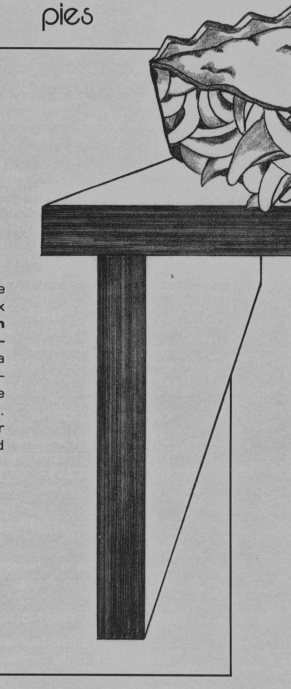

A PEACH OF A PIE

5 large ripe **peaches**
3 tablespoons **flour**
4 tablespoons **brown sugar**

Slice the **peaches** into a bowl. Sprinkle with **flour** and **brown sugar** and mix well. Place the peaches around a **frozen pie crust** and dot with **butter** and **apricot preserves.** Bake in a pan or on a cookie sheet or aluminum foil. The ingredients tend to overflow the crust, and we wouldn't want to mess up your oven. Bake at 450° for 10 minutes, then lower to 400° for 20 minutes. Cool, slice and serve.

pies

CHOCOLATE BAR PIE
—A SUPER-SWEET CRAVING

Since the Munchies can strike at any moment, and since they may manifest themselves as a super-sweet craving, bear in mind that this particular recipe should be prepared in advance.

1 **chocolate bar**—5-ounce
8 regular size **marshmallows**
¼ cup **milk**
½ pint **heavy cream**
1 **pie shell**

Melt the **chocolate bar** and **marshmallows** in **milk** in a double boiler and cool. Whip the **heavy cream** and mix with the chocolate and marshmallows. Pour into a **baked pie shell** and chill in the refrigerator for at least 2 hours. Before consuming, pour on more **whipped cream** and sprinkle with a handful of **chocolate chips.**

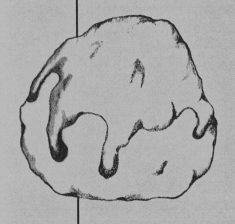

TIPPIE'S PUFFS

Melt 1 stick **margarine** with 1 cup **water** in a pot until they start to boil. Stir 1 cup **flour** into the boiling mixture until it makes a smooth thick paste. Pour into a pot or bowl and refrigerate 5 or 10 minutes. After the mixture is coolish, take 3 large **eggs** and beat in one at a time. Drop heaping tablespoons of the dough on an ungreased cookie sheet and bake at 400° for 30 minutes till light and fluffy and golden brown.

TIPPIE'S FROSTING FOR TIPPIE'S PUFFS

Mix 1 cup **confectioners' sugar** with the juice of 1 **lemon** until very thick and pasty. Spread on the puffs.

MESSAGE: Pastry can be cut open and filled with anything, strawberries and whipped cream, or, if the frosting is left off, sauces or meats.

CREAM CHEESE ICING WITH CHOCOLATE CHIPS FOR A YELLOW OR WHITE CAKE WHICH CAN BE HOMEMADE OR STORE-BOUGHT.

Beat an 8-ounce package of **cream cheese** with 1 teaspoon **vanilla** and 1½ cups **milk** until smooth. Throw in a handful of **chocolate chips** and spread on your cake.

INSTANT STRAWBERRY SHORTCAKE

Toast a piece of **pound cake** and top it off with thawed **frozen strawberries, whipped cream** and **walnuts.**

puddings

YOUR OWN THING, UPSIDE-DOWN, SWEET POTATO PUDDING

Take a pie pan and cover the bottom most generously with **butter.** Sprinkle with 4 tablespoons of **brown sugar** and arrange the contents of a small can of **pineapple rings** and some **maraschino cherries.** You can cut up the rings or halve the cherries to spell out your name or that of a loved one. Try a self-portrait or your favorite landscape. But don't spend too long, because there is more to do. Mash 1 medium-size can of **sweet potatoes** with 2 capfuls of **brandy flavoring** and ¼ cup **heavy cream.** Mix well and pour over the pineapple rings and cherries and bake for about 45 minutes at 350°.

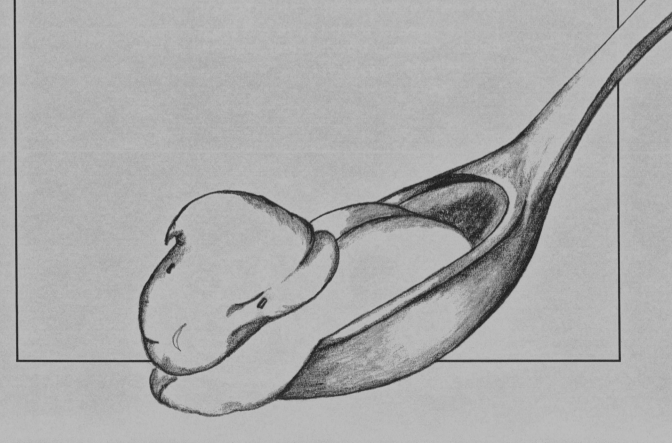

puddings

A COCONUT PUDDING

Beat 2 **eggs** and add 2 tablespoons **sugar,** 4 tablespoons **flour** and ¼ cup **raisins.** Gradually pour in 2 cups **milk** and then add 1 cup **shredded coconut,** ½ teaspoon **vanilla** and ¼ teaspoon **salt.** Pour into a shallow baking pan and bake in a 350° oven for about 45 minutes. Top with **heavy cream** or **whipped cream.**

CHOCOLATE RICE PUDDING WITH RAISINS AND COCONUT

Cook 1 package of either **instant** or **regular chocolate pudding** according to directions, adding 1 capful of **almond extract.** When cooked, take off heat and add 1 cup of **cooked rice** and a handful of **softened raisins***. Pour into individual bowls and eat either hot or cold.

* see page 31 for the definition of **softened raisins**

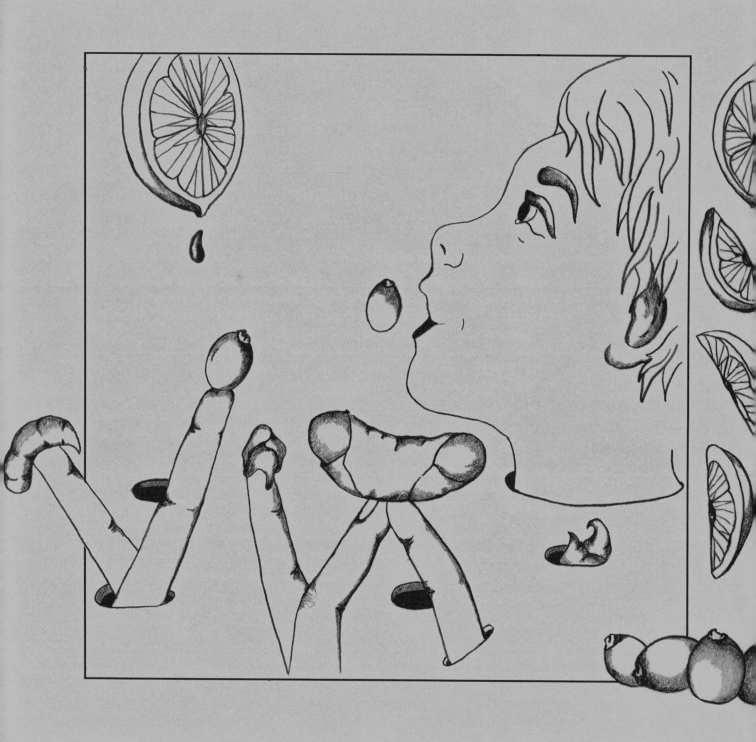

salty, spicy, sour and other cravings

Following in the footsteps of Sweet, come Salty, Spicy, Sour and other cravings. Although not as popular, they are flavors not to be overlooked or laughed at. Appearing together here for the first time, they are for use whenever the Munchies take their form.

individual quickies

PROCEDURAL INSTRUCTIONS AND SUGGESTIONS FOR THE ASSEMBLY AND SATISFACTION OF INDIVIDUAL QUICKIES

1. Place all parts in front of you in order of assembly. (Read individual quickies instructions.)

2. Practice the procedure indicated until your dexterity is perfected.

3. Once assembly is perfected, speed up the assembly time.

4. When you feel you are ready, enter into competition with a friend.

5. To make competition interesting, frequently change the order of assembly or change the position of parts keeping the same assembly procedure.

6. **FOR CHAMPIONS ONLY.** Mix the parts from two or more individual quickies and assemble.

MESSAGE: Although we emphasize the speed of assembly, we don't suggest that the individual quickies should be consumed with the same exuberance. Once assembled, please take your time and savor the flavor.

individual quickies

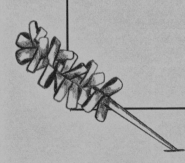

These individual quickies may be assembled and eaten immediately.

Spear a cube of **pineapple,** a cube of **cheddar cheese** and a **maraschino cherry.**

Spear a cube of **american cheese,** a **walnut half** and a **sweet pickle.**

Wrap a slice of **ham** around **apple** cubes and dip in **mayonnaise.**

Wrap a slice of **roasted sweet red pepper** around a cube of **swiss cheese** and sprinkle with **parmesan cheese.**

Spear a cube of **smoked cheese,** then a **grape.**

Spear a cube of **apple,** dip it in **wine** or **lemon juice** and then roll it around in a **sharp cheese spread.**

These individual quickies must be assembled and then heated as directed.

Wrap a cube of **pineapple** with a slice of **corned beef,** dip in either **grape jelly** or **orange marmalade** and put in the oven until hot.

Wrap a slice of partially cooked **bacon** around a **pineapple chunk** and put in broiler until bacon is done.

Spread **potato chips** on a cookie sheet. Sprinkle with grated **cheddar cheese** and heat in oven till cheese melts.

What one uses to transport a flavorful dip from its container to one's mouth is called a DIPPER. When choosing a dipper, remember that the flavor of the dip and the texture of the dipper should always be in accord with the cravings of your mouth. Experimentation with different combinations of dips and dippers brings about the state of the PEACEFUL PALATE.

crackers	**carrot sticks**	**pineapple chunks**
cookies	**tomato wedges**	**apple wedges**
potato chips	**celery sticks**	**peach slices**
pretzels	**cucumber wedges**	**cooked shrimp**
corn chips	**scallions**	and, of course,
french fries	**raw broccoli**	your **fingers**

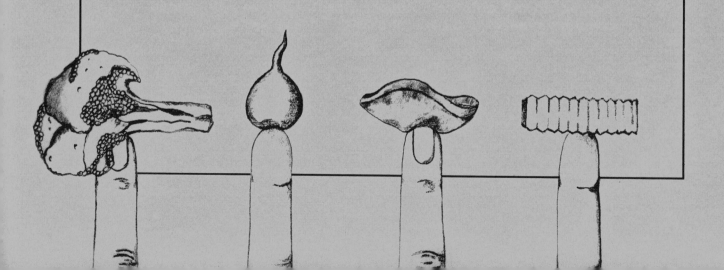

dips

PEANUT BUTTER AND KETCHUP

Mix an equal amount of **peanut butter** and **ketchup** until smooth and then sink your dipper way down deep.

CHILI AND TUNA

Combine an individual-size can of **tuna** with a small bottle of **chili sauce.** Add about ½ teaspoon of **chili powder** and a good squeeze of **lemon juice.** Skim the top of this dip with your dipper.

QUICK DIP

Combine a ½ pint of **sour cream** with ½ a package of **cheese-garlic salad dressing mix.** Stir in a little **salt** and a few drops of **hot sauce.** Position your dipper high above the dip bowl, then plunge quickly and directly into the dip.

OLIVE-CHEESE WITH NUTS

Mix a ½ pint of **creamed cottage cheese** with a few tablespoons of grated **cheddar cheese,** some sliced **ripe olives, chopped walnuts** and **salt.** This dip really tastes good on fingers.

flavored butters

This page is dedicated to those who feel there is more than one way of having your bread buttered.

Mix softened **butter** with the other ingredients and blend thoroughly.

HONEY BUTTER—¼ cup soft **butter**, ¼ cup **honey**.

HAM BUTTER—¼ cup soft **butter**, ¼ pound diced **ham**, 1 **hard-boiled egg** chopped fine.

PIZZA BUTTER—¼ cup soft **butter**, 2 tablespoons **chili sauce**, ½ teaspoon **oregano**.

PARMESAN BUTTER—¼ cup soft **butter**, 2 tablespoons grated **parmesan cheese**.

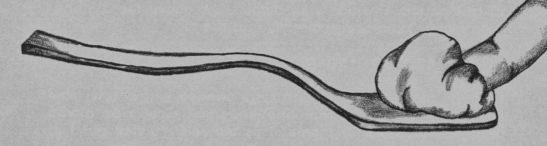

OLIVE-WALNUT BUTTER—¼ cup soft **butter**, ½ cup chopped **ripe olives**, ½ cup **chopped walnuts**.

MUSTARD BUTTER—¼ cup soft **butter**, 1 tablespoon prepared **mustard**.

GARLIC BUTTER—¼ cup soft **butter**, 1 clove pressed or chopped **garlic** or ½–¾ teaspoon **garlic powder** to taste.

SESAME BUTTER—¼ cup soft **butter**, 2 tablespoons **sesame seeds**.

mixed bag

HERE ARE TWO FOR YOU FROM SUE

#1 SUPER SHELLS

Bake frozen **pastry shells** according to directions. After baking, fill them with a heated mixture of chopped **cooked chicken** or **turkey** and a can of undiluted **cheese soup** or a can of **newburg sauce**. You can also add **nuts, peas** or **water chestnuts.**

#2 MOON ROLLS

Before baking a package of refrigerated **crescent rolls,** spread with a **sharp cheese spread** and fill with **tuna** or **cocktail franks.** Roll up and bake as directed.

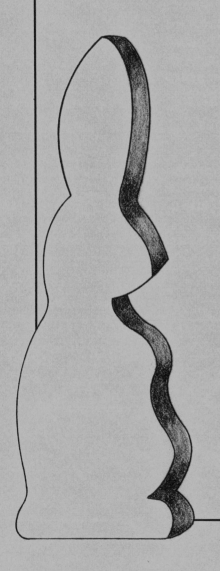

HOT PARMESAN TOASTIES

Chop ½ an **onion,** add ½ cup **mayonnaise** and 6 tablespoons grated **parmesan cheese.** Mix everything together and spread liberally on lightly toasted **white** or **whole wheat bread.** Cut the bread into quarters, eighths, angels, gingerbread men, ducks or bunny rabbits. Broil till brown, bubbly and delicious.

HOT WHEELS

Trim the crust from a slice of **white** or **whole wheat bread.** Roll out the bread thin and spread with a mixture of ¼ cup grated **cheddar cheese** and 2 tablespoons **chili sauce,** then roll up jelly-roll style. Cut into ½″ slices, dot with **butter** and broil until brown.

mixed bag

A WACKY SNACK

Mix 1½ cups of **cooked rice** with ½ stick of soft **butter** or **margarine,** 1 **egg,** 3 tablespoons grated **parmesan cheese** and **salt** and **pepper.** Blend all ingredients and form a ball of the mixture about the size of a rubber ball, small apple or large plum. Push a chunk of **mozzarella cheese*** into the center of the ball and fry in about 1″ of hot **oil** until light brown. * You can also add **sausage, pepperoni, anchovies,** etc., to the chunk of cheese.

PICKLE POWER

Stack a slice of **sharp cheese,** a slice of **raw onion** and a slice of **sour pickle** on an **onion cracker.** Spread with **hot mustard** and eat immediately. Repeat the process until either the ingredients run out or you get full.

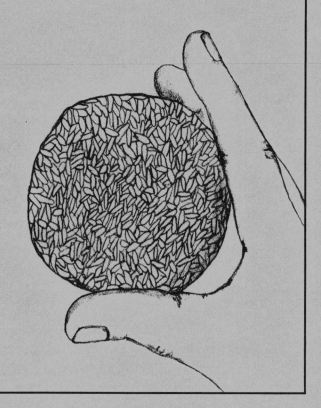

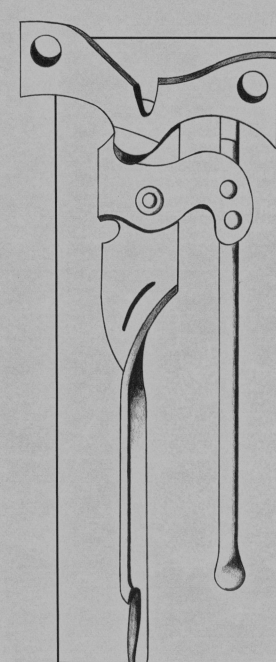

METHODS FOR MAKING MARTIN'S MANY MAGNIFICENT SOUPS

Make canned soup according to directions and then add:

To **cream of mushroom soup:** Some leftover **chicken** and a can of **whole kernel corn.**

or A can of **tuna fish** and some **cooked mixed vegetables.**

To **cream of chicken soup:** Some leftover **chicken** or **turkey** and a can of **lobster** or **crab meat.**

To **cream of tomato soup:** A blob of **sour cream** mixed with **chives.**

To **cream of potato soup:** A can of **tuna fish** and cubes of **ham.**

COLONEL SOUP

Dilute one medium can **creamed corn** with ¾ cup **milk.** While heating add a little **flour,** some **onions** and some **ham.** Also try with other things you like.

soups

TOMATO SOUP, WHIPPED CREAM AND CHEDDAR CHEESE

Mix a can of **tomato soup** with **milk** as indicated on the soup can. Combine an equal amount of **unsweetened whipped cream** and grated **cheddar cheese.** Pour soup, either hot or cold, into a mug, and spoon on the whipped cream and cheese mixture. **Salt** and **pepper** to taste.

OPTIMUM ONION SOUP

Make 1 package **instant onion soup mix** according to directions. Sauté 1 large **onion** in **butter** in a saucepan and add to soup. Divide evenly in ovenproof soup bowls. Cover with 2 layers of **gruyere cheese** and top that with a layer of **buttered white toast** cut into quarters. Add 2 layers of **swiss cheese** and 2 more **gruyere cheese.** Bake at 475° for about 10 minutes or until slightly browned and bubbling. Sprinkle with lots of grated **parmesan cheese** and eat.

eggs

CHOPPED EGGS AND ONIONS— A BOWLFUL

Chop together 3 medium size **onions** and 6 **hard-boiled eggs.**
Tastes best when you add about 4 tablespoons of **chicken
fat.** You can also use **mayonnaise** if chicken fat is not your
thing. Season with lots of **salt.**

NOODLES AND ONIONS IN SCRAMBLED EGGS

Fry **onions** in **butter** till brown. Add **cooked noodles** and a
couple of **eggs** beaten with a little **milk.** Fry all together, slide
onto a plate, pour on some **ketchup.**

EGGS, TOMATOES AND CHEESE
. . . OH MY!

Cut and fry 1 **tomato** in **butter** till soft.
Add 4 **eggs** beaten with a little **milk,**
pieces of **swiss cheese** or **cheddar
cheese** and **salt** and **pepper.** Cook to
desired doneness.

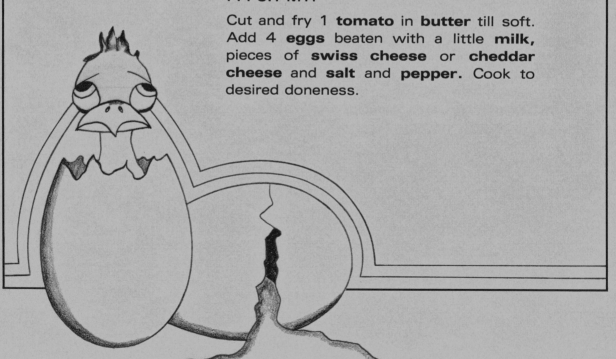

eggs

OPULENT OMELET

Beat together 2 **eggs,** ¼ cup **milk** or **cream** and a pinch of **salt** and **pepper.** Melt **butter** in a frying pan and pour the mixture in. Let the bottom get a little brown, then flip over and lay 2 slices of **american cheese** on top. While the bottom side is getting brown, the cheese on top will melt. Fold up both ends of the omelet toward the center, remove from the pan and eat.

You can put **jelly** or a few slices of **cooked bacon** or a few tablespoons of heated, undiluted **vegetable soup** in the center of the omelet before folding for an added treat.

SCRAMBLED EGGS AND CHOCOLATE SYRUP

Be the first one on your block to try some **chocolate syrup** over your favorite **scrambled eggs.** It will give you a new oral experience and a reputation for trying anything at least once.

vegetable goodies

PRIMO PATTIES

Mash the well-drained contents of 2 medium-size cans of **mixed vegetables** together with 4 ounces of **instant mashed potato flakes, 2 eggs, salt** and **pepper.** Form patties and fry in about 1″ of hot **oil** until brown. Flip over and brown other side. Serve with a can of undiluted **cream of mushroom soup** mixed with a little **milk** and heated slightly, as a **sauce.**

ROLLED AND FRIED STRINGBEANS

Break fresh **stringbeans** into bite-size pieces. Dip in an **egg** beaten with a little **salt,** then roll around in **bread crumbs** and fry in **shortening, butter** or **oil** until brown. Drain on a **paper napkin** and eat.

TOMATO TINGLERS

Cut a **tomato** in half, then sprinkle with **salt** and **pepper.** Blend **mayonnaise, grated onion** and **parmesan cheese** together and spoon on each tomato half. Broil until mayonnaise mixture is bubbly.

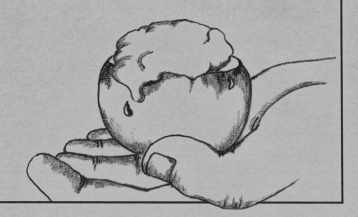

vegetable goodies

OLD-FASHIONED POTATO PANCAKES

Peel and grate 6 medium **potatoes** and 1 medium **onion.** Drain excess liquid from mixture, then add 5 **eggs, salt** and **pepper.** Mix everything together and pour by tablespoons into hot **oil** in a frying pan. Fry until brown on both sides. Serve with **applesauce, jelly, sugar** or **sour cream.** Makes plenty and is well worth the trouble.

MUSHROOMS AND ONIONS

Fry **mushrooms** and **onions** in **butter.** Season with **salt, garlic** and **basil.** Add **white wine** while cooking for an ultimate taste sensation.

HOT TOMATOES

Scoop out the insides of a few **tomatoes** and mix with **flavored bread crumbs, sugar, salt, pepper** and **curry powder** to taste. Restuff the tomatoes, dot with **butter** and sprinkle with grated **parmesan cheese.** Broil for 15 minutes, cool slightly, then consume.

salads

Many Munchers are satisfied
successfully by bowls of
crispy colorful combinations of
various vital vegetables or
fancy flavorful fruits. These
mixtures are commonly called
Salads. The Munchies make
these Salads uncommonly
delicious.

AUTHOR'S NOTE:

It is our opinion that fruits have a decidedly happy quality, while vegetables are definitely serious.

We think this is true because in those days of yesteryear, dear old Mom loudly and sternly demanded that you "Eat your vegetables, they're good for you." This gave vegetables a very serious connotation. Anything being good for you must be serious. Fruits very rarely reached that pinnacle of importance in Mother's heart.

As you remember, being a kid you always did the opposite of what Mom wanted and what was good for you anyway. So, while vegetables remained a serious topic, fruits were reserved for those free happy times when you weren't reminded of what was good for you and what wasn't.

You're probably asking what relevance this all has to the Munchies. Our answer is that we wish to reinstate vegetables in the hearts and minds of all those people alienated by childhood remembrances. You must block out those echoing voices of old, stammer up determination and will power and munch a raw carrot or a handful of fresh shelled green peas. Not only will your Munchies be surprisingly satisfied, but by preparing your salad and getting into the patterns, shapes and colors of the various ingredients, your other senses will also be delightfully entertained.

LOVELY LEAVES, FRENCH DRESSED

Make a nice bowl of bite-size pieces of **lettuce, watercress** and **spinach leaves.** Grate a **carrot,** slice some fresh **mushrooms,** chop a few **scallions** and toss in. Dress lightly but completely with your favorite **french dressing.**

BUFFY'S SALAD BOWL

Tear up a head of **lettuce** and mix with raw **cauliflowerets,** fresh shelled **green peas, plum tomatoes** and **green pepper** strips. Mix some **crushed pineapple** with **french dressing** and pour over everything.

GLORIOUS GREENS WITH ONION RINGS

Put **lettuce** and **spinach leaves** in a bowl. Crush some canned **onion rings** on top, add a sprinkling of **sprouts*** and toss with **salad oil** and **cider vinegar** mixed with **basil** and **rosemary.**
* **Sprouts** are certain seeds that have been exposed to heat and moisture in one of various methods, producing the start of new growth. They are very healthy and very delicious in salads.

VARIATION ON A COMMON THEME

Slice a **cucumber,** a **tomato,** an **onion,** a **green pepper** and some **radishes** into whatever sizes and shapes you feel are indigenous to their munchability. Combine with **lettuce leaves** in a large bowl, **salt** and **pepper** to taste and add:

american cheese slices or **pineapple chunks**
ham cubes **bacon bits**
pine nuts **walnuts**
corn chips **raisins**

dress with:

dress with:

mayonnaise and **ketchup** mixed until it looks a deep salmon color. Add a little **milk, garlic powder** and **pickle relish.** If you want, **chopped egg** adds a great taste.

yogurt mixed with an equal amount of **applesauce** and sprinkled with lots of **cinnamon.**

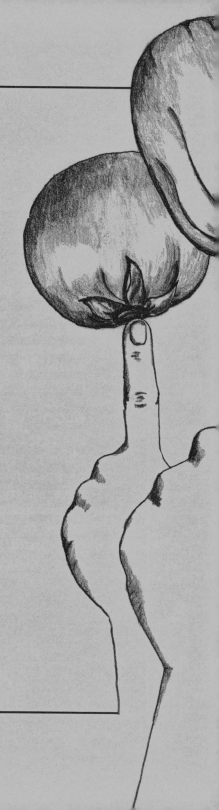

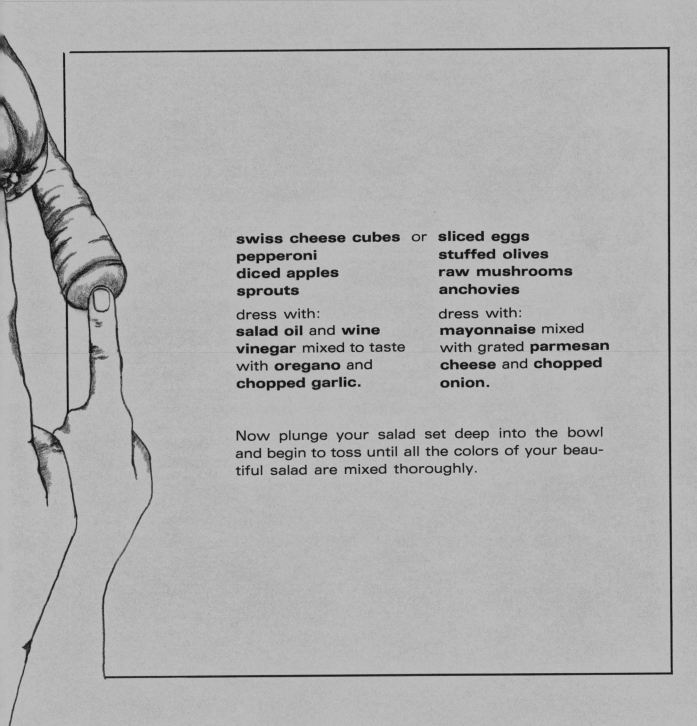

swiss cheese cubes or **sliced eggs**
pepperoni   **stuffed olives**
diced apples   **raw mushrooms**
sprouts   **anchovies**

dress with: dress with:
salad oil and **wine**   **mayonnaise** mixed
vinegar mixed to taste   with grated **parmesan**
with **oregano** and   **cheese** and **chopped**
chopped garlic.   **onion.**

Now plunge your salad set deep into the bowl
and begin to toss until all the colors of your beautiful salad are mixed thoroughly.

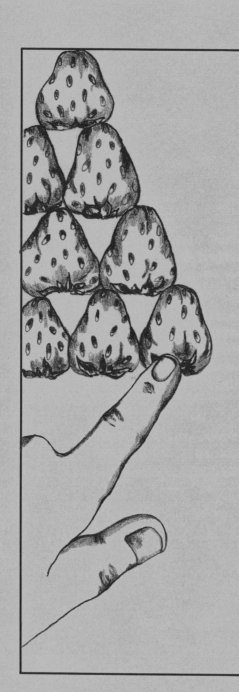

STRUNG-OUT STRAWBERRIES

Combine **avocado** wedges with **orange** and **grapefruit** sections and sliced **bananas** in a bowl. Carefully place fresh whole **strawberries** side by side around the edge of the bowl and sprinkle everything with **powdered sugar.**

A REAL COOL SALAD

Make a mixture of **cantaloupe** slices, **pineapple chunks, orange** sections, **seedless grapes** and **blueberries** in a large bowl. Scoop out a generous amount of **lemon sherbet** and mix with the fruit. Eat only one piece of fruit at a time until all are gone. Then spoon the sherbet left in the bottom of the bowl into your waiting mouth.

YOU CAN HAVE IT BOTH WAYS SALAD

Mix **pineapple rings, bing cherries,** a bunch of **seedless grapes** and sliced fresh **strawberries.** Cover them either with **cottage cheese** and **sour cream** mixed with **cinnamon, sugar** and **chopped walnuts,** or **cream cheese** blended with a little **milk,** some grated **cheddar cheese, chopped pecans** and **sugar.**

ULTIMATE FRUIT SALAD

Combine the well-drained fruit from a small can each of **fruit cocktail, mandarin oranges** and **pineapple chunks.** Toss in lots of **maraschino cherries,** a handful of **miniature marshmallows** and a sprinkling of **shredded coconut.** Mix thoroughly with a pint of **sour cream** and refrigerate for about an hour. If you can't wait that long, devour immediately.

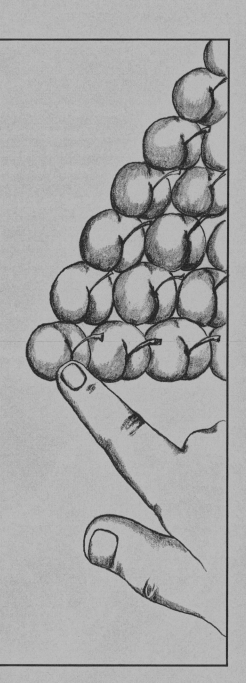

ORANGE, ONION AND OLIVE SALAD

Combine **sweet onion** slices with **orange** sections and large **ripe olives** on a carpet of **lettuce**. Spill **french dressing** mixed with **sprouts** over everything.

AN ORANGE-FLAVORED BANANA SALAD

Cut a **banana** into small pieces and dip in **orange juice.** Put drained banana into a bowl with **red cabbage** and **escarole** and mix with **mayonnaise** and **whipped cream** blended in equal amounts.

CHERRIES, GRAPES AND WALNUTS

Mix **bing cherries, seedless grapes** and **shelled walnuts** in a bowl. Spoon **sour cream** blended with a little **orange juice** and **shredded coconut** on top.

FRUIT SALAD JAMBOREE

Assemble, in a bowl lined with **lettuce,** 3 sliced **apples,** 3 sectioned **oranges,** a handful of **sesame** or **sunflower seeds, chopped nuts** and **raisins.** Toss with **mayonnaise,** covering all members generously.

APPLES, AVOCADOS AND APRICOTS

Slice 2 **apples,** 2 **avocados** and 2 **apricots** and arrange by alternating slices of each in a bowl with **spinach leaves** and a handful of **seedless grapes.** Mix **honey** and **lemon juice** with **sour cream** and spoon on top.

APPLE-CARROT-RAISIN-CELERY-WALNUT SALAD

Make a medley of diced **apples,** sliced **carrots, raisins,** diced **celery** and **chopped walnuts.** Mix together with **mayonnaise, salt, pepper** and lots of **cinnamon.** Present on **lettuce** or **watercress.**

TUNA TRILOGY

#1 TUNA TRIAL

Mix a can of **tuna** with **mayonnaise,** lots of grated **apple, cinnamon** and **chopped walnuts.**

#2 TOOTHSOME TUNA

Mix a can of **tuna** with **mayonnaise,** diced **celery** and chopped **onion, sweet pickle** and **hard-boiled eggs.**

#3 TUNA TRIUMPHANT

Mix a can of **tuna** with **mayonnaise,** sliced **water chestnuts** or slivered **almonds, raisins, basil, dill** and **chives.**

SHRIMP AND COMPANY

Combine diced **celery,** 1 sliced **sour dill pickle,** 1 sectioned **orange,** 2 sliced **carrots** and about a dozen cooked **shrimp.** Toss with **mayonnaise** mixed with **tarragon.**

TROPICAL SEAFOOD SALAD

For the tropical part of this salad, cut 2 **bananas,** 2 **avocados** and a few **pineapple rings** and place in a bowl of your favorite **salad greens.** Sprinkle with ½ cup of **lemon juice.** For the seafood part, add about a dozen cooked **shrimp.** Cover liberally with **french dressing** mixed with **toasted sesame seeds.**

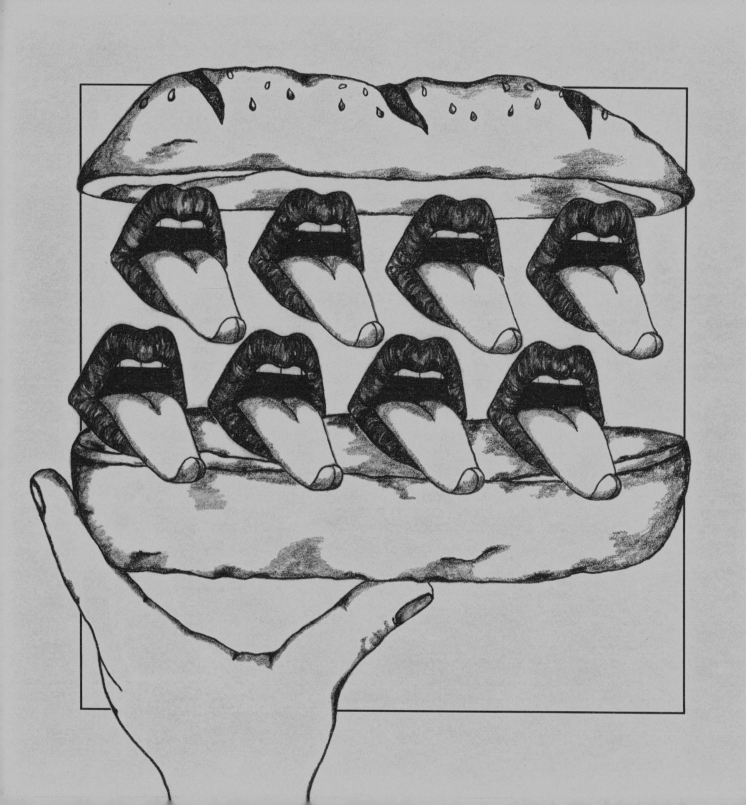

sandwiches

Sandwiches, like other
pleasures in life, demand
variation for complete and
total satisfaction. Therefore,
we now give you 50
MUNCHIE MARVELS.

HOW TO PICK A MUNCHIE MARVEL

As you will notice, the **50 MUNCHIE MARVELS** are each numbered. It has been our experience that when the Munchies strike and a sandwich becomes the vehicle for satisfaction, a lack of decisiveness as to what sandwich to make, can cause a disconcerting feeling called oral frustration. Therefore, rather than inflicting this unpleasant affliction upon yourself, we suggest the following:

Randomly pick a number from 1 to 50. Add the total amount of toothbrushes in the bathroom and divide by 2. This will give you a number. Find the corresponding numbered sandwich, prepare and eat.

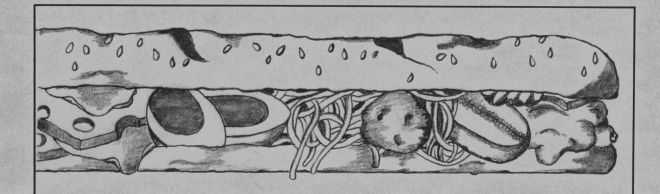

or   Compute the total playing time of your favorite record album to the nearest minute, divide by your shoe size and add the last digit of your telephone number.

or   Add together the number of the day you were born with the number of times you've regretted it. If more than 50, divide by 2. If more than 100, try another method of calculation, you're too depressed to use this one.

If mathematics was never one of your best subjects, just start at 1 and progress through 50, noting your favorites in case of future oral frustrations.

1. Tender **turkey roll,** with thin slices of **swiss cheese,** topped with lots of **mayonnaise, salt** and **pepper,** between two thick slices of **rye bread.**
2. Hot **turkey slices,** smothered with **cranberry sauce,** on a **seeded roll.**
3. **Turkey slices,** covered with **russian dressing** and topped with **lettuce, tomato slices** and grated **cheddar cheese,** on **white toast.**
4. **White bread,** spread with **mayonnaise** and **mustard** topped with a slice of **ham, apple slices** and **american cheese,** then broiled until the cheese melts.
5. **Ham** slices, covered with a layer of **potato salad** on **white bread** and fried in **butter** until brown.

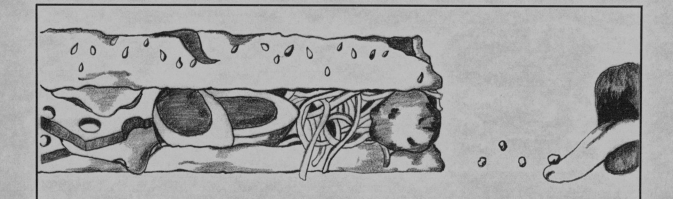

6. Thin slices of **ham,** covered with thin slices of **swiss cheese** and a juicy **pineapple ring** sprinkled with **brown sugar,** all on one half a lightly toasted **english muffin,** broiled until the cheese bubbles.

7. Sliced **virginia ham,** covered with **pineapple preserves,** on a **seeded roll.**

8. **Roast beef,** sliced thick and fried in **butter,** arranged on **white toast** covered with **mayonnaise, lettuce** and **tomato.**

9. Sliced **roast beef,** covered with **russian dressing,** a layer of **swiss cheese, lettuce** and a nice healthy slice each of **raw onion** and **tomato,** all on a **seeded roll.**

10. Sliced **roast beef,** bathed in **gravy** and smothered with **mashed potatoes,** on a **hard roll.**

11. Lean **corned beef,** covered with **sauerkraut, russian dressing** and a layer of **swiss cheese,** on **buttered black bread** and heated in the oven until the cheese is melted.

12. Alternating layers of thin sliced **corned beef** and **cheddar cheese,** topped with **hot mustard** and **pimento pepper strips,** on **rye bread.**

13. **Smoked tongue** and **swiss cheese,** spread with **salad mustard** and topped with a **tomato** slice, on a **hero roll.**

14. **Ham bologna,** covered with sliced **hard-boiled eggs** topped with lots of **ketchup,** on **buttered whole wheat bread.**

15. **Bologna** and sliced **sour pickles,** covered with thin-sliced **swiss cheese** spread with a spoonful of **mayonnaise,** on a **hot seeded roll.**

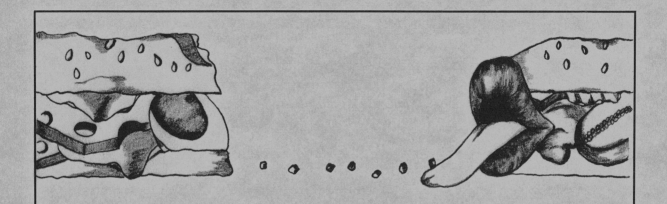

16. Slices of **liverwurst,** covered with **grape jelly,** on **white bread.**

17. One half an **english muffin,** covered by slices of **italian salami** drenched with **tomato paste** and a layer of **mozzarella cheese** sprinkled with **oregano** and broiled until the cheese melts.

18. Slices of **italian salami** and **mozzarella cheese,** topped with **green pepper strips,** between slices of **buttered french bread,** grilled until bread is toasty.

19. Sliced, **cooked italian hot sausage,** covered with **spaghetti sauce** and thin slices of **mozzarella cheese** and baked until hot, then laid in the center of a heated **hero roll.**

20. **Italian salami** spread with **cream cheese,** on a **seeded onion roll.**

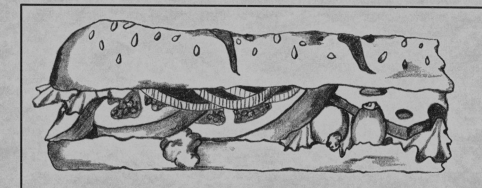

21. Cold **meat loaf,** doused with **ketchup** or **chili sauce,** on **buttered white bread.**
22. **Peanut butter, orange marmalade** and a thin slice of **cheddar cheese,** on **white toast.**
23. **Peanut butter,** covered with **applesauce** and **bacon bits,** on **whole wheat toast.**
24. **Peanut butter, marshmallow creme** and **banana** slices on **toasted cinnamon raisin bread.**
25. Your choice of **jelly** spread on **buttered white toast,** with a slice of **american** or **swiss cheese** melted on top.

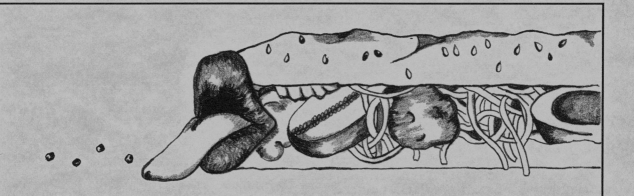

26. **Grape jelly** on **buttered white toast,** topped with slices of **banana.**
27. **Anchovies, cream cheese** and sliced **pimento-stuffed olives** on **white toast.**
28. Sliced **olives, cream cheese** and **raisins** on **pumpernickel bread.**
29. **Cream cheese** blended with **honey** and **chopped walnuts** on **whole wheat bread.**
30. One half a toasted **english muffin** spread with **cream cheese** and **chives** and topped with a small jar of **shrimp cocktail.**

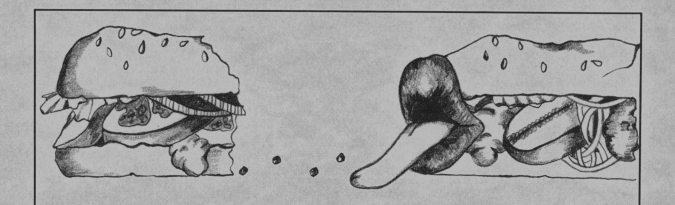

31. **Cream cheese** blended with **maraschino cherries** and a little **vanilla extract,** spread liberally on **white bread.**

32. **Cream cheese** mixed with **chopped walnuts** on thick slices of **date nut bread.**

33. **Cream cheese** and fresh **blueberries** sprinkled with **sugar** on **sprouted wheat bread.**

34. A **toasted bagel** sliced in half, with **cream cheese** liberally spread on both halves, covered with a layer of **nova scotia salmon, onions,** a slice of **tomato** and small sliced **pimento-stuffed olives.**

35. Canned **salmon** mixed with diced **onion, lemon juice** and **mayonnaise,** spread on one half a lightly toasted **english muffin,** then broiled a few minutes.

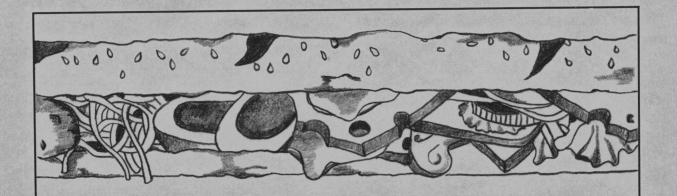

36. Melted **american cheese** on **raisin bread** spread with **tuna salad***. (*see page 68 for **tuna salad** recipes)
37. **Tuna salad** on a slice of **buttered whole wheat toast,** topped with a layer of **swiss cheese,** broiled until the cheese melts.
38. **Sardines** sprinkled with a squeeze of **lemon,** lying on a bed of **lettuce,** topped with slices of **onion** and **tomato,** on **white toast** spread with **mayonnaise.**
39. **Sardines** sprinkled with **lemon juice,** covered with thin slices of **hard-boiled egg,** on **buttered white toast.**
40. **Sardines** topped with slices of **sweet pickle** on **buttered whole wheat bread.**

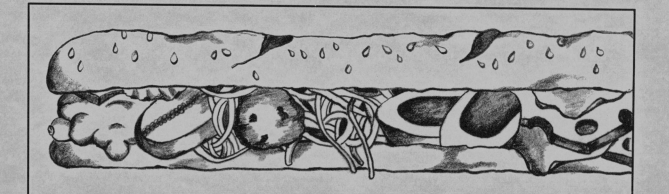

41. A **fried egg** sprinkled with **salt** and covered with **ketchup,** on a **hard roll** brushed with the drippings from the frying pan.

42. Sliced **hard-boiled egg** topped with a layer of **roasted sweet pepper** on **buttered whole wheat toast.**

43. **Instant onion soup mix** combined with **sour cream** and **salad shrimp** on **white toast** with **lettuce.**

44. A lightly toasted **buttered english muffin** topped with a slice of **tomato,** an **onion** slice and a layer of **american cheese,** then broiled until the cheese melts.

45. **Rye bread** spread with **sour cream** and **mustard,** topped with sliced **radishes, cucumbers** and **onions.**

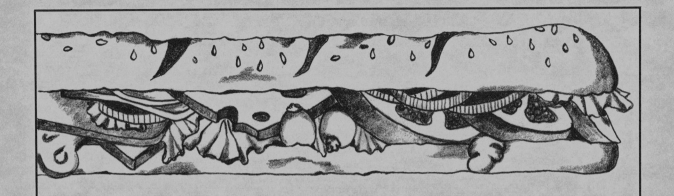

46. Sliced **cucumbers** sprinkled with **black pepper** and **salt** on **white bread** spread with **mayonnaise.**

47. **Fried mushrooms** (fresh are better, but canned still work) and **onions,** topped with **bacon slices,** on a **seeded hard roll.**

48. **Baked beans, brown sugar, onion** and **bacon bits,** heated and thickly spread on **buttered rye bread.**

49. Sliced **frankfurters** and **sweet pickles,** on a heated **roll.**

50. **Applesauce** mixed with a generous amount of **cinnamon,** covered by a slice of **american cheese,** all between two slices of **white bread,** then pan-fried in **butter** until the cheese melts.

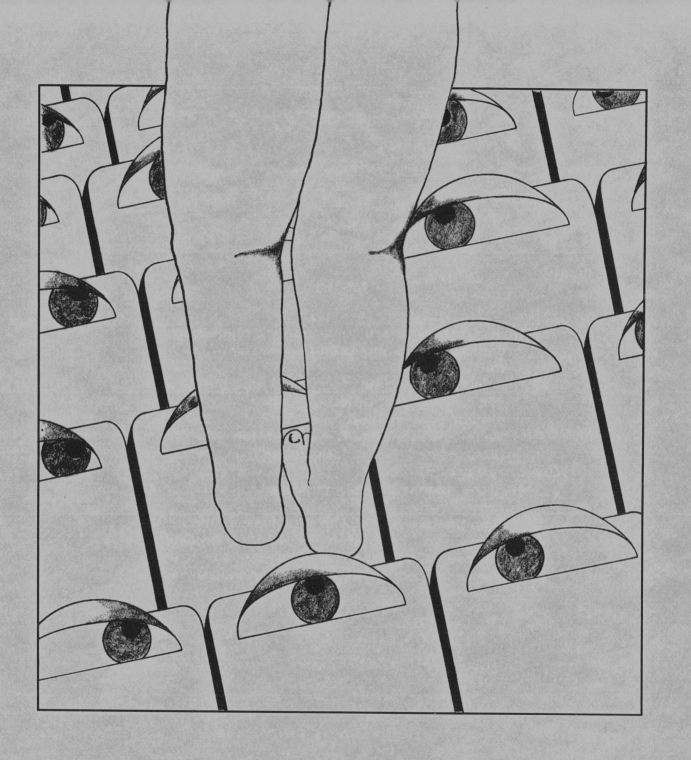

chapter 6

Do you shyly scrutinize your bathroom scale every morning? Do you make it a point to hang all the mirrors in your house behind doors you never open? Does your beautiful belly feel a bit bulgy? Do you now have the Munchies?

We understand your problem and have written these recipes with you in mind. We wouldn't want you to gorge yourself on fattening fancies or broadening beverages. Therefore, eat what you want from what we've presented, so that you may feel fully contented.

watching your weight

HESS HINTS FOR HELPING HEAVIES

1. Use low-calorie substitutes wherever they apply.

2. Keep lots of fresh vegetables on hand.

3. Substitute plain yogurt whenever sour cream is called for.

4. Don't read the Sweet Cravings chapter in this book.

5. Place the most fattening things in your refrigerator in the back, making them difficult to remove.

6. Adjust your bathroom scale to read 10 pounds heavier; you won't feel like eating so much.

7. Eliminate all visions of sugarplums dancing in air.

8. Close your eyes and cover your ears when the food commercials appear on the television.

9. Pursue a policy of non-involvement with your cookie jar.

10. Remember how it feels to be heavy on your heels.

COMFORTING CANTALOUPE

Cut half a **cantaloupe** into bite-size cubes and place gently in a bowl. Fill a juice glass about ¾ full of **orange juice** and a few drops of **rum extract.** Proceed by forking a melon cube and dipping it slowly into the juice mixture. When the melon is coated, remove from the glass and deposit in your mouth. Repeat the process, one melon cube at a time, until they are all gone. Then drink the juice, wipe your mouth, rub your stomach and repeat over and over, "Boy, am I full."

MELTED MEDLEY FOR TWO

Core and slice 1 **apple** into quarters. Cut 1 **peach** into quarters and remove the pit. Neatly lay all fruit on a baking pan and sprinkle with **cinnamon.** Divide 1 slice each of **american** and **swiss cheese** into quarters and alternate the different cheeses, on top of the different fruits, until all 8 cheese pieces cover all 8 fruit quarters. Bake until cheese melts. Now separate the medley equally between two plates, thereby preventing you or your eating partner from partaking of more than the 4 delicious cheese-fruit combo's that you each are entitled to. If, however, you wish to abide by the honor system, only one plate will be necessary.

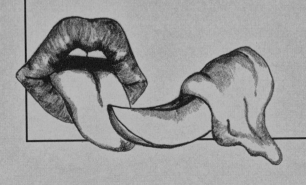

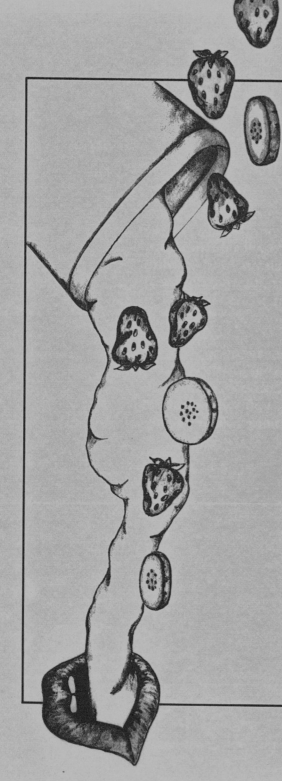

YUMMY YOGURTS

SWEET BERRIES

Combine ½ cup **plain yogurt** with ½ cup fresh **strawberries** and 2 teaspoons **honey**.

CRUNCHY BANANA

Combine ½ cup **plain yogurt** with ½ a sliced **banana**, 2 teaspoons **brown sugar** and 2 tablespoons of **wheat germ**.

CUCUMBER AND MINT

Combine 1 cup **plain yogurt**, 1 sliced medium **cucumber**, 2 teaspoons of crushed **mint** and **salt** to taste.

SPICED TOMATO

Combine 1 cup **plain yogurt**, 1 or 2 sliced **green onions**, 1 small cubed **tomato**, 1 tablespoon **basil** and **salt** to taste.

ANGEL APPLE ANGEL

Whipped-cream cakes are definitely out. There-fore, for your pleasure, cut a homemade or store-bought **angel food cake** in half lengthwise. Make a mixture of unsweetened **applesauce** and **cin-namon** to taste and spread thickly between the two layers of cake. Let the applesauce mixture soak into the fluffy white cake and then cut your-self a piece and enjoy.

APPLE-COLA

Pour 4 ounces of chilled **unsweetened apple juice** into your glass. Fill completely with an ice-cold **low-calorie cola soda** and float a slice of **lemon** or **lime** on top.

BUTTERMILK WITH BUBBLES

Combine an equal amount of cold **buttermilk** and a **low-calorie cream soda**. Add 1 large **ice cube,** stir and sip.

FRUIT SHAKE FROST

Mix ¼ cup **orange juice,** with ¼ cup **apple juice,** 2 tablespoons cold **skim milk** and ½ teaspoon **vanilla extract.** Put in blender until smooth, then add 3 **ice cubes** one at a time until each is well crushed.

COCOA COFFEE COOLER

Blend 1 cup cold **skim milk** with 1 teaspoon **instant coffee powder**, 2 teaspoons **unsweetened cocoa powder**, 1 tablespoon **brown sugar** and ½ teaspoon **vanilla extract**. Pour into your glass, sip and savor.

PEACH SHAKE

Add 1 cup cold **skim milk** to ¼ cup canned-in-water **peach slices**, 2 teaspoons **brown sugar,** ½ teaspoon **rum extract** and a few **ice cubes.** Blend until smooth and frosty.

FRUIT JUICE FONTANA FORTUNE

Combine 1 cup each of chilled **orange juice** and chilled **unsweetened pineapple juice** and add a few drops of **rum extract** for additional delicious flavoring.

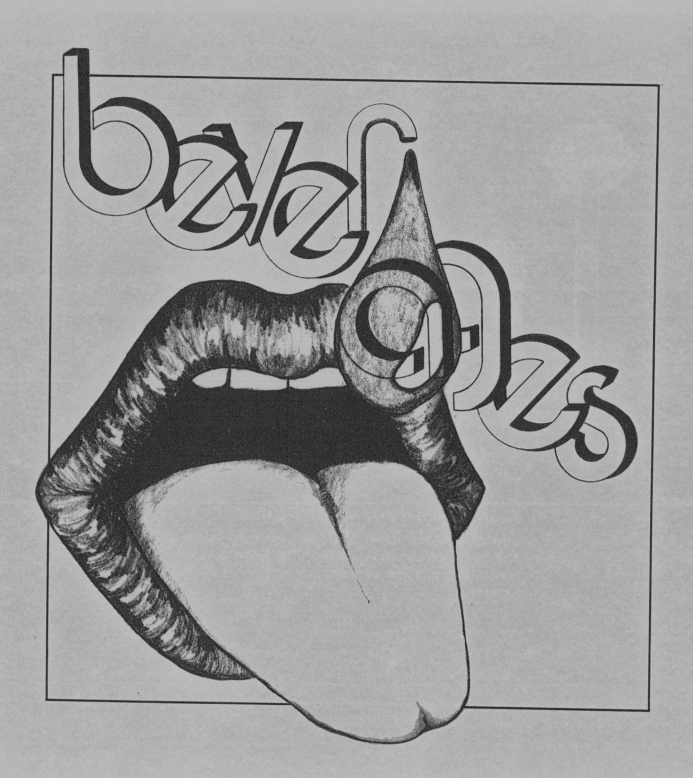

chapter 7

beverages

Munchies can sometimes manifest themselves as thirsts. When a Munchie thirst strikes, you may be engaged in any one of innumerable different, intensely engrossing occupations. Therefore we have coordinated our Munchie Thirst Satisfiers with familiar situations to which we feel they are appropriate. Thusly, we now present THIRTY-THREE THOROUGHLY THIRST-QUENCHING THOUGHTS.

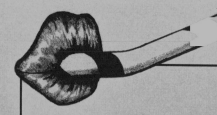

1. Dancing divinely with a daredevil driver, while daintily downing a **DOUBLE-DIP DINGER**.

   DOUBLE-DIP DINGER: Combine 1 cup of **milk** with ¼ cup **strawberry syrup**. Add 2 large scoops of **vanilla ice cream** and fill to the top with **club soda**.

2. Randomly running, boyishly barefooted, through a florid field of dank dandelions, while dreamily drinking a **BLOOMIN' BLENDED BANANA**.

   BLOOMIN' BLENDED BANANA: Mix 1 cup of **milk,** a **banana,** peeled and sliced, 1 heaping tablespoon **honey** and **maraschino cherries** and **juice.** Blend until smooth and creamy.

3. Sitting by the fireside, following flickering flames, while systematically sipping a SIZZLING CINNAMON CIDER.

SIZZLING CINNAMON CIDER: Heat 1 cup of **apple cider** with a couple of **cinnamon sticks** until warm. Pour into your mug with an additional **cinnamon stick** as a stirrer.

4. Sweetly savoring a majestic mug of GARDEN GLORY, while whimsically watching your geraniums germinate.

GARDEN GLORY: Heat canned **vegetable juice cocktail.** While heating, stir in grated **cheddar cheese.** Pour into your mug, sprinkle with **chives** and top with a pat of **butter.**

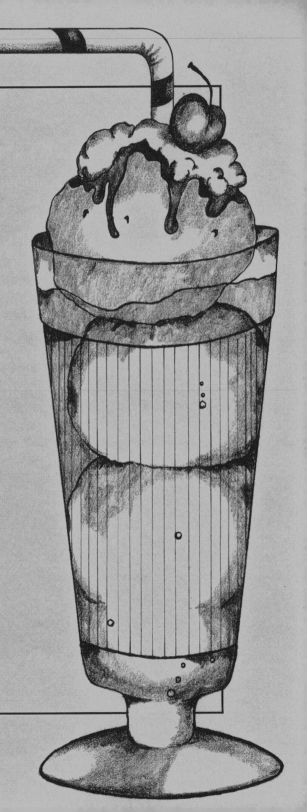

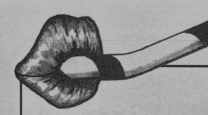

5. Fancifully following a fly down Fifth Avenue, while gaily gulping a **NEW YORK EGG CREAM.**

   NEW YORK EGG CREAM: Cover the bottom of your glass with about 1 inch of **chocolate syrup.** Add about another inch of **milk** and fill the rest of the glass with **seltzer water** or **club soda.** Stir and gulp.

6. Playing ping-pong with a prudent playmate, while periodically passing a **PEACH PASSION.**

   PEACH PASSION: Mix 1 cup of **milk** with 2 teaspoons **brown sugar,** a pinch of **salt,** some **crushed ice** and a few **peach slices.** Whirl in a blender until smooth.

7. Wildly waving on your water bed, while wantonly wassailing with a **WET WHISTLE**.

   WET WHISTLE: Combine an equal amount of chilled **white wine** and **peach nectar**. Add a few sliced **peaches** and blend.

8. Sitting on a sundeck on a sunny summer Sunday, while silently sipping a **SUN-KISSED SOOTHER**.

   SUN-KISSED SOOTHER: Put 2 large scoops of **vanilla ice cream** in your glass and fill with **orange juice**.

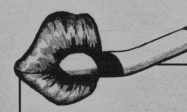

9. Placidly playing with the feathers falling from your plush pillow, while neatly nursing a glass of **WARM MAPLE MILK.**

   WARM MAPLE MILK: Stir **maple syrup** into a glass of **warm milk** to taste. Drop **maraschino cherries** into the glass for a pleasant reward when you finish all your milk.

10. Rakishly reaching for a **ROUSING RUM** while restfully reclining after a rollicking romance.

    ROUSING RUM: Blend 2 ounces of **orange juice,** 1 ounce of **lime juice** and 2 teaspoons **sugar** with **dark rum** to taste. Float an **orange slice** on top as an added palate pleaser.

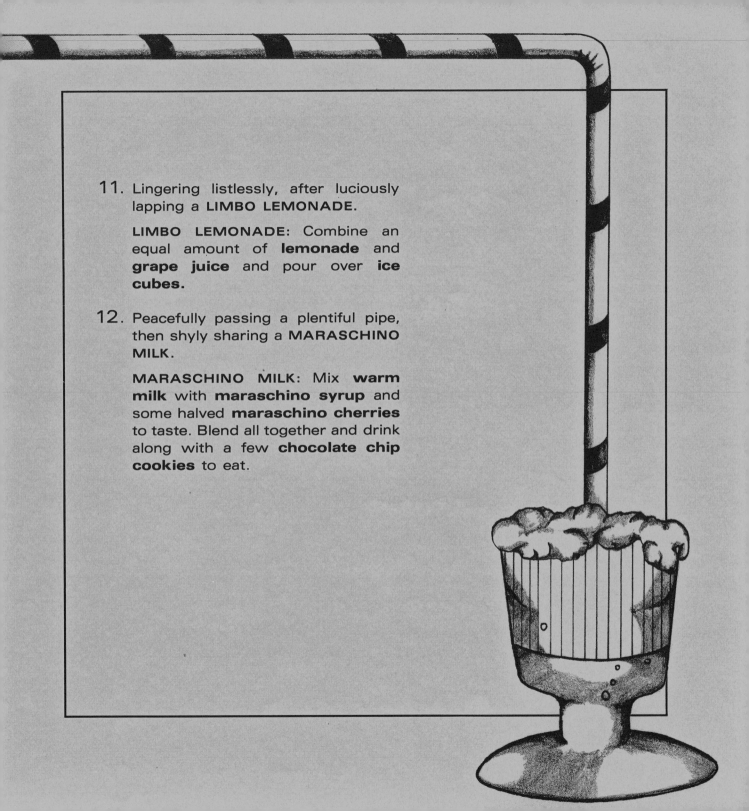

11. Lingering listlessly, after luciously lapping a **LIMBO LEMONADE**.

    LIMBO LEMONADE: Combine an equal amount of **lemonade** and **grape juice** and pour over **ice cubes.**

12. Peacefully passing a plentiful pipe, then shyly sharing a **MARASCHINO MILK**.

    MARASCHINO MILK: Mix **warm milk** with **maraschino syrup** and some halved **maraschino cherries** to taste. Blend all together and drink along with a few **chocolate chip cookies** to eat.

13. Playfully pushing a plump plum with your prominent proboscis, then fervently filling your babbling belly with a **BANANA BOUNTY.**

   BANANA BOUNTY: Blend 1 cup of **milk** with **banana liqueur** to taste. Add a few **banana slices** and some **crushed ice** and blend again.

14. Adoringly adulating the amorous adventures of your audacious Airedale, while sweetly sipping an **APHRODITE APRICOT.**

   APHRODITE APRICOT: Combine ½ cup of chilled **apricot nectar** with 1 cup **milk,** 1 tablespoon **sugar** and 1½ teaspoons **lemon juice** in your glass and sip.

15. Ravenously raiding a resplendent refrigerator for refreshment, then raggedly retiring with a pitcher of **POTLUCK POTION.**

    POTLUCK POTION: Unite 1 cup **milk,** 1 **egg,** 1 tablespoon **sugar,** 1 teaspoon **vanilla** and a few sliced **strawberries.** Blend and drink.

16. Making Munchie meals of marshmallow and marmalade, while successfully satisfying your thirsty throat with a **NAIROBI NOG.**

    NAIROBI NOG: Blend 1 sliced **banana** with a couple of large scoops of **vanilla ice cream,** 1 cup **milk,** 1 **egg** and 1 teaspoon **vanilla extract.** Sprinkle with **nutmeg.**

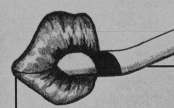

17. Tempestuously toasting two terribly titillating teetotalers with a **TOLEDO TINGLER**.

TOLEDO TINGLER: Pour ½ cup **grapefruit juice,** ¼ cup **orange juice** and ¼ cup **pineapple juice** into your glass. Spill **club soda** gently into the mixed fruit juices and float a slice of **lemon, lime** or **orange** on top.

18. Rapping repetitiously with a raving righteous radical, then reaching rather restlessly for a **REACTIONARY REFRESHER**.

REACTIONARY REFRESHER: Blend 4 tablespoons of **crushed pineapple** with 1 tablespoon **sugar,** 1 ounce **light rum** and a few drops of **mint extract.** Fill your glass with **cracked ice** and pour the mixture in. Then refresh and relax.

19 . Entirely entranced by the exuberant entrance of an engaging eyeful, while waiting wolfishly for a gurgling glass of **GENTLEMAN'S GINGER**.

GENTLEMAN'S GINGER: Pour 4 ounces each of **apricot nectar** and **unsweetened pineapple juice** in your glass. Fill slowly with **ginger ale** and float a slice of **lemon** on top.

20 . Hobnobbing with a hip haberdasher from Hoboken, while happily having a **HOPALONG HONEY**.

HOPALONG HONEY: Spoon a heaping tablespoon of your favorite **honey** into a coffee mug. Fill your cup halfway with **hot coffee** and then fill completely with **milk**.

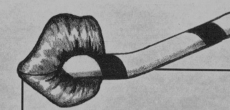

21. Soliciting scent of sea lion and being invited in for a **CANDY COCOA**.

   CANDY COCOA: Spoon 2 tablespoons of **chocolate syrup** into your mug. Add **warm milk** and stir with a **peppermint stick**.

22. Persistently pursuing a playful prospect for a passionate performance, while pleasingly partaking of a **PALATE PROMISE**.

   PALATE PROMISE: Blend 1 peeled and sliced **banana** with 2 large scoops of **vanilla ice cream,** 1 cup **milk** and 2 tablespoons of **frozen lemonade concentrate**.

23 . Lovingly laddling a **LOCO LEMON-ADE** down your lithesome larynx.

LOCO LEMONADE: Fill your favorite wine glass with an equal amount of ice-cold **lemonade** and chilled **dry red wine.**

24 . Cautiously conversing with a curious collector of culinary cravings, while cozily coddling a **CHOCO-LATE COFFEE**.

CHOCOLATE COFFEE: Spoon 2 tablespoons of **chocolate syrup** into your mug. Add **hot coffee** and 1 tablespoon **sugar.** Top with **whipped cream** or **miniature marshmallows.**

25. Gleaning guides of gastronomic goodies for guaranteed gratifiers, while guzzling a goblet of **GLACIER GRAPEFRUIT, GRAPE AND PEACH.**

GLACIER GRAPEFRUIT, GRAPE AND PEACH: Freeze **grapefruit juice, grape juice** and **peach nectar,** in cubes, in separate ice-cube trays. Place 2 cubes of each flavor in your glass. Pour **ginger ale** gently down the side of the glass and wait for the different flavors to melt and mingle.

26. Flagrantly flaunting your favorite flask filled with the flavorful fluid, **FRUITY FRAPPE.**

FRUITY FRAPPE: Mix 1 cup of **milk** with ¼ cup **sweetened pineapple juice** and 2 large scoops of **vanilla ice cream.** Blend till smooth, then fill your flask.

27. Quickly quenching a quarrelsome quandary with quaffs of quintessence of **QUININE AND ORANGE.**

QUININE AND ORANGE: Blend 6 ounces of **quinine water** with 4 ounces **orange juice** and 1 tablespoon **vanilla-flavored syrup.** Pour into your glass, drop in a couple of **ice cubes,** a **maraschino cherry** and float a slice of **orange** on top.

28. Calmly considering constructive criticism at your counterculture convocation, while soothingly sipping a **SANGUINE SODA.**

SANGUINE SODA: Mingle the flavor of **vanilla cream soda** with that of **milk** to taste. Or if you prefer, **chocolate cream soda** and **milk.**

29 . Contentedly caressing a certain cigarette of coverted contents, while consuming cups of **CARRIBEAN COFFEE SHAKE.**

CARRIBEAN COFFEE SHAKE: Blend a few large scoops of **chocolate ice cream** with ½ cup **milk** and 2 tablespoons **coffee flavored liqueur.**

30 . Doing devious deeds on her daddy's divan, while deliriously downing a **DURANGO DELIGHT.**

DURANGO DELIGHT: Mix ½ cup of **orange juice** with ½ cup **buttermilk** and 1 table-spoon **honey.** Blend till smooth, pour into your glass and sprinkle with **nutmeg.**

31. Blithely bathing in balmy banana bubbles, while calmly caressing a gurgling glass of **LOCKE LIMEADE.**

LOCKE LIMEADE: Cut a fresh **lime** in half and squeeze the juice into the bottom of your glass. Add 3 or 4 tablespoons of **vanilla-flavored syrup** and fill the glass completely with **seltzer water** or **club soda.** If your taste runs sweeter, add more vanilla syrup. If sour, more lime.

32. Delightedly dosing a dizzy damsel with a diabolical **DEVIL'S DUE.**

DEVIL'S DUE: Mix ½ cup **sweet wine** with ¼ cup **water** and heat. Pour into your mug and stir in 2 teaspoons of **maple syrup.** Top with a pat of **butter** and sprinkle with **cinnamon.**

33. Cleverly constructing allusive alliterations, while poignantly partaking of an **ALBUQUER-QUE APPLE SHAKE.**

ALBUQUERQUE APPLE SHAKE: Peel and core a medium-size **apple** and cut into small cubes. Combine with 1 cup **milk,** 2 teaspoons **brown sugar,** 2 tablespoons **honey** and **cinnamon.** Blend until your shake is delightfully thick and frothy.

index

index

index

index

index

index

Alice and Eliot Hess are creative partners in their own design studio in Brooklyn, New York. Their work has included adventures in writing, illustration, photography and film. Eliot studied architecture at Pratt Institute and photography at the School of Visual Arts, where Alice was studying design and illustration. This, their first book, is a perfect combination of their artistic talents and enormous appetites.